PRINCEWILL LAGANG

Walking the Path Together: Christian Marriage Advice

First published by PRINCEWILL LAGANG 2023

Copyright © 2023 by Princewill Lagang

All rights reserved. No part of this publication may be reproduced, stored or transmitted in any form or by any means, electronic, mechanical, photocopying, recording, scanning, or otherwise without written permission from the publisher. It is illegal to copy this book, post it to a website, or distribute it by any other means without permission.

Princewill Lagang asserts the moral right to be identified as the author of this work.

First edition

This book was professionally typeset on Reedsy.
Find out more at reedsy.com

Contents

1. Walking the Path Together: Christian Marriage Advice — 1
2. The Foundation of Christian Marriage: Love and Faith — 4
3. Nurturing Your Christian Marriage through Communication and... — 7
4. Weathering Life's Storms: Christian Marriage and Trials — 10
5. Parenting with Purpose: Raising Children in a Christian... — 13
6. Building Strong Foundations: Financial Stewardship in... — 16
7. Intimacy and Purity in Christian Marriage — 19
8. Weathering Life's Seasons: The Beauty of Aging Together — 22
9. A Legacy of Love: Leaving a Lasting Impact — 25
10. A Journey of Endless Discovery: Nurturing Your Christian... — 28
11. Looking Back and Looking Forward: A Journey of Reflection... — 31
12. Love that Never Fades: The Legacy of a Christian Marriage — 34

1

Walking the Path Together: Christian Marriage Advice

The Journey Begins

In a quiet, sunlit room, the soft hum of a ceiling fan blended with the sweet melodies of birdsong that filtered through an open window. The room was adorned with symbols of faith, from a beautifully crafted cross on the wall to a well-worn Bible perched on a wooden nightstand. It was in this sanctuary of love and devotion that Sarah and David prepared to embark on the most significant journey of their lives - their Christian marriage.

Sarah sat on the edge of their shared bed, her delicate hands trembling as she adjusted the delicate lace veil that graced her auburn hair. Her heart raced with a mix of excitement, anticipation, and just a touch of nervousness. She looked at herself in the ornate mirror opposite, a smile playing at her lips as her eyes caught a glimpse of her soon-to-be husband, David, standing in the doorway.

David was a sturdy man, with a presence that radiated strength and gentleness in equal measure. He watched Sarah with an expression of awe, his hazel eyes sparkling with love and admiration. As Sarah caught his gaze, her earlier anxiety melted away, replaced by the profound assurance of the love they shared.

Sarah and David were deeply committed Christians, both having grown up in faith-based families and having nurtured their own spirituality throughout their lives. Their marriage was not just a union of hearts, but a partnership in faith. The journey they were about to embark upon would not only intertwine their lives but would also be guided by the principles and values that their Christian faith held dear.

As Sarah and David took their first steps down the aisle, the congregation of friends and family watched in reverence. The air was charged with the sense of something sacred, a union that extended far beyond mere earthly commitments. They were embracing the divine covenant of marriage, guided by the profound teachings of Christ, who exemplified love, compassion, and the selflessness that would underpin their journey together.

The beauty of Christian marriage is that it's not just a union of two individuals, but a merging of two paths, two sets of values, and two spiritual journeys. Their shared faith was the foundation upon which their love was built, and the beacon that would light their way through life's darkest moments.

As they stood before the altar, they exchanged their vows, promising to love and cherish each other in the sight of God and their community. It was not just an exchange of words; it was a commitment to walk the path together, side by side, through all the joys and trials that lay ahead. Their marriage was rooted in faith and guided by principles that had withstood the test of time, offering them solace and wisdom in every challenge they would encounter.

This book, "Walking the Path Together: Christian Marriage Advice," is a journey through the sacred institution of Christian marriage. It is a guide for couples who seek to build their lives together with faith as their cornerstone. In the chapters that follow, we will explore the wisdom and guidance that

Christianity offers to couples on their marital journey. We will delve into the scriptures, reflecting on the teachings of Christ, and discover how they can enrich and strengthen your marriage.

As Sarah and David concluded their wedding ceremony, they stepped forward into the grand adventure of married life. In that sacred moment, they understood that their Christian faith was not a spectator in their relationship but an active participant, an ever-present guide that would help them navigate the many twists and turns on the path ahead.

This book is an invitation to every Christian couple to embrace their faith as a source of strength, wisdom, and inspiration in their marriage. As we journey together through these pages, may you discover the profound beauty of "Walking the Path Together" in Christian marriage, where love and faith intertwine to create a union that is truly blessed.

2

The Foundation of Christian Marriage: Love and Faith

Building a Love that Lasts

Love is the cornerstone of Christian marriage. In the grand tapestry of human emotions, it stands as the most profound and the most sacred. It is through love that we connect with God's divine purpose, as articulated in 1 Corinthians 13:4-7: "Love is patient, love is kind. It does not envy, it does not boast, it is not proud. It does not dishonor others, it is not self-seeking, it is not easily angered, it keeps no record of wrongs. Love does not delight in evil but rejoices with the truth. It always protects, always trusts, always hopes, always perseveres."

In Christian marriage, love is not just an emotion but a commitment—a choice made every day. It is a love that reflects the boundless love of Christ for His Church, a love that forgives, endures, and seeks the well-being of the beloved.

The Commandment of Love

In Matthew 22:37-39, Jesus gave us the greatest commandment: "Love the

Lord your God with all your heart and with all your soul and with all your mind. This is the first and greatest commandment. And the second is like it: 'Love your neighbor as yourself.'"

For a Christian couple, this means not only loving each other deeply but also living out this love in their daily lives. It's about treating each other with the same love and respect that Christ showed to all, regardless of circumstances. Love in marriage becomes a reflection of God's love, a living testimony to the world of what it means to love as Christ loved us.

Walking the Path Together

The path of love and faith in Christian marriage can be both enchanting and challenging. It's a journey that requires intentionality, prayer, and unwavering faith. Here are some practical steps to help you build a love that will stand the test of time:

Prayer: Prayer is a powerful tool for building and strengthening your love. Regularly pray together as a couple. Seek God's guidance, wisdom, and blessings for your marriage.

Communication: Open and honest communication is essential. Listen to your partner with love and understanding. Remember the words of James 1:19, "My dear brothers and sisters, take note of this: Everyone should be quick to listen, slow to speak and slow to become angry."

Forgiveness: In a world that often promotes a "me-first" attitude, embrace the power of forgiveness. Colossians 3:13 tells us, "Bear with each other and forgive one another if any of you has a grievance against someone. Forgive as the Lord forgave you."

Selflessness: Put your partner's needs before your own. Philippians 2:3-4 advises, "Do nothing out of selfish ambition or vain conceit. Rather, in humility, value others above yourselves, not looking to your own interests but each of you to the interests of the others."

Quality Time: Spend quality time together. Make it a priority to nurture your relationship, creating special moments and shared experiences.

Community: Engage with your church community and seek support and counsel when needed. Ecclesiastes 4:9-10 reminds us, "Two are better than one because they have a good return for their labor. If either of them falls down, one can help the other up. But pity anyone who falls and has no one to help them up."

Faith in Action: Lastly, remember that love without action is hollow. In 1 John 3:18, it is written, "Dear children, let us not love with words or speech but with actions and in truth."

The path of love in Christian marriage is illuminated by faith. It's a path where every step is taken in the light of God's love, where every challenge is met with the resolve to love as Christ loved us. In the pages that follow, we will delve deeper into the practical aspects of nurturing love and faith in your Christian marriage, drawing inspiration from Scripture and the wisdom of generations of faithful couples who've walked this path before you.

3

Nurturing Your Christian Marriage through Communication and Connection

Building Bridges of Understanding

Marriage, even when blessed by Christian faith, is not immune to the challenges and misunderstandings that arise from daily life. Communication, the lifeblood of any healthy relationship, plays a pivotal role in a Christian marriage. It is through open and honest communication that you build bridges of understanding, strengthen your bond, and face challenges with grace.

The Power of Words

The Bible provides profound wisdom on the power of words. Proverbs 18:21 reminds us that, "Death and life are in the power of the tongue." In a Christian marriage, words can be instruments of healing or harm, tools of love or destruction. It's vital to choose words carefully, and to do so in love.

Active Listening

Effective communication isn't just about speaking; it's also about listening. The Apostle James urges us to be "quick to listen and slow to speak" (James 1:19). Actively listening to your partner means giving them your full attention, empathizing with their feelings, and understanding their perspective. It's a way to show respect and love.

Conflict Resolution

Disagreements are inevitable in any marriage. In a Christian marriage, the focus should be on resolving conflicts in a way that honors your faith and the commitment you've made. Ephesians 4:26-27 advises, "In your anger, do not sin: Do not let the sun go down while you are still angry, and do not give the devil a foothold." This verse encourages you to address issues promptly and with love, seeking reconciliation rather than harboring resentment.

Quality Time Together

Building a strong Christian marriage also involves spending quality time together. In the busyness of life, it's easy to neglect this aspect, but it's crucial for maintaining a strong connection. Ecclesiastes 9:9 reminds us to "enjoy life with your wife whom you love all the days of this meaningless life that God has given you under the sun." Make time for each other, create cherished moments, and keep the flame of love burning bright.

Shared Spiritual Life

A Christian marriage is deeply enriched when you share a spiritual life together. Praying together, attending church, and discussing matters of faith can deepen your bond. Ecclesiastes 4:12 speaks of the strength of a cord of three strands, representing the unity of husband, wife, and God. Together, you can find spiritual guidance, grow in faith, and strengthen your commitment to each other and to God.

Nurturing Trust

Trust is a foundational element of a strong Christian marriage. Proverbs 31:11 tells us, "The heart of her husband trusts in her, and he will have no lack of gain." Trust is built through consistency, honesty, and faithfulness. It's a reflection of the trust you place in each other and, ultimately, in God.

Grace and Forgiveness

Forgiveness is a cornerstone of the Christian faith, and it's equally vital in a Christian marriage. Ephesians 4:32 encourages us to "Be kind to one another, tenderhearted, forgiving one another, as God in Christ forgave you." Extend grace and forgiveness to each other, just as God has forgiven you.

In a Christian marriage, communication and connection form the bedrock of a loving and faith-driven partnership. As you continue your journey, remember that every conversation, every moment of connection, is an opportunity to build your love, nurture your faith, and fortify the bonds that make your union sacred. In the chapters ahead, we will explore more ways to enrich your Christian marriage, drawing from the wellspring of Christian wisdom and love.

4

Weathering Life's Storms: Christian Marriage and Trials

Anchored in Faith Through Life's Challenges

The path of Christian marriage is not always bathed in perpetual sunshine. Like any other journey, it encounters its share of storms and challenges. However, the foundation of faith upon which Christian marriages are built equips couples to weather these storms with unwavering love and resilience.

Trials in Marriage

Trials can take many forms. Financial difficulties, health issues, family disputes, and personal crises can test the strength of a marriage. A Christian marriage, rooted in faith, possesses the spiritual resilience to face these trials with grace.

Prayer in Times of Trial

James 5:13 encourages us to "Is anyone among you suffering? Let him pray." Prayer is an essential tool in seeking God's guidance, strength, and comfort during difficult times. In a Christian marriage, prayer together is a way of drawing closer to God and to each other.

Support from Your Christian Community

Lean on your Christian community for support during trying times. Galatians 6:2 implores us to "Carry each other's burdens, and in this way, you will fulfill the law of Christ." Your brothers and sisters in Christ can offer counsel, encouragement, and the love you need to navigate challenges.

Turning to Scripture for Guidance

The Bible is a wellspring of wisdom and guidance for couples facing trials. 2 Corinthians 4:8-9 assures us, "We are hard-pressed on every side, but not crushed; perplexed, but not in despair; persecuted, but not abandoned; struck down, but not destroyed." Scripture can provide comfort and direction during difficult times, reminding you that God is your refuge and strength.

Resilience Through Unity

Trials can either weaken or strengthen a marriage, depending on how you navigate them. A Christian marriage can emerge from trials even stronger, as you face adversity united by your faith and love for one another. Romans 8:28 reassures us that "in all things, God works for the good of those who love Him." This promise extends to your marriage as well.

A Testimony of Faith

Your Christian marriage is a living testimony of your faith in Christ. When you face trials with unwavering love and trust, you demonstrate the power of faith to the world. 1 Peter 1:6-7 encourages us, "In all this, you greatly rejoice, though now for a little while you may have had to suffer grief in all kinds of trials. These have come so that the proven genuineness of your faith—of greater worth than gold, which perishes even though refined by fire—may result in praise, glory, and honor when Jesus Christ is revealed."

The Role of Forgiveness

During trials, it's crucial to forgive and support each other. Colossians 3:13 reminds us to "Bear with each other and forgive one another if any of you has a grievance against someone. Forgive as the Lord forgave you." Forgiveness can be a healing balm for your relationship during challenging times.

Persevering in Faith

Perseverance is a key virtue in facing trials as a Christian couple. Hebrews 12:1 encourages us to "run with perseverance the race marked out for us." Persevere in your marriage, knowing that God is with you every step of the way.

In a Christian marriage, trials are not seen as insurmountable obstacles, but as opportunities to grow in faith and love. As you continue to walk this path together, remember that God's grace and your unwavering love for each other will help you weather life's storms. The next chapters will delve deeper into the specific challenges you may encounter and how your faith can guide you through them.

5

Parenting with Purpose: Raising Children in a Christian Marriage

Guiding the Next Generation in the Way of Faith

The journey of Christian marriage often includes the profound responsibility of parenthood. Raising children in a Christian home is a sacred duty, and it brings unique challenges and joys. In this chapter, we explore how Christian couples can navigate the complex and rewarding role of parenting while keeping faith at the heart of their family life.

The Gift of Children

Children are often described in the Bible as a blessing from God. Psalm 127:3 tells us, "Children are a heritage from the Lord, offspring a reward from Him." Recognizing this, Christian parents have the opportunity and responsibility to nurture the faith of the next generation.

Teaching by Example

Christian parents should be the living embodiment of faith, demonstrating the principles and values of Christianity in their daily lives. Your children will learn more from what they see you do than from what you tell them. Ephesians 6:4 advises, "Fathers, do not exasperate your children; instead, bring them up in the training and instruction of the Lord."

Prayer and Worship as a Family

Praying and worshiping together as a family is a powerful way to cultivate a Christian home. It reinforces the importance of faith in your lives and helps your children develop their own relationship with God. Deuteronomy 6:6-7 says, "These commandments that I give you today are to be on your hearts. Impress them on your children. Talk about them when you sit at home and when you walk along the road, when you lie down and when you get up."

Education in Faith

In a Christian home, education extends beyond academics to the teaching of faith. Proverbs 22:6 reminds us, "Start children off on the way they should go, and even when they are old, they will not turn from it." Christian parents can provide their children with a strong moral and spiritual foundation through scripture and teachings of Christ.

Guiding Through Challenges

Christian parenting is not without its trials. The world can present conflicting values and temptations. James 1:5 advises, "If any of you lacks wisdom, you should ask God, who gives generously to all without finding fault, and it will be given to you." Turn to God for guidance when facing difficult decisions about your children's upbringing.

Encouraging Questions

Welcome and encourage questions from your children about faith. Engaging in conversations about Christianity can strengthen their understanding and allow them to develop a personal connection with God.

Nurturing Love and Grace

Just as in your marriage, extend love and grace to your children. 1 Corinthians 16:14 teaches, "Do everything in love." Show love and understanding, even when addressing their mistakes and guiding them back to the path of faith.

Seeking Support

As Christian parents, you don't have to journey alone. Your church community can be a valuable source of support and guidance. Share your challenges, seek advice, and build a network of fellow Christian parents who can help you navigate the path of parenthood.

In a Christian marriage, parenting is an extension of the partnership in faith you've built with your spouse. Together, you can raise children who understand the importance of faith, who embrace Christian values, and who seek to walk the path of Christ. Your family can become a beacon of light and love, illuminating the way for future generations. As you continue to raise your children in the way of faith, remember that your love, your teachings, and your example will leave an indelible mark on their hearts and souls.

6

Building Strong Foundations: Financial Stewardship in Christian Marriage

Faithful Management of Resources

In Christian marriage, the management of finances is more than a practical concern; it is a matter of stewardship and faith. Money can be a source of both blessing and conflict, and it is essential to establish strong financial foundations that align with your Christian values.

The Spiritual Perspective on Finances

1 Timothy 6:10 teaches, "For the love of money is a root of all kinds of evil." Money itself is not inherently good or evil; it's how we approach and manage it that determines its impact. In a Christian marriage, money is viewed as a resource to be managed wisely and in a way that honors God.

Shared Financial Goals

A successful financial partnership begins with shared goals and values. Open and honest discussions about your financial aspirations, such as savings, charitable giving, and long-term plans, can provide a solid foundation for your financial journey.

Budgeting as a Couple

Proverbs 21:5 reminds us that, "The plans of the diligent lead to profit as surely as haste leads to poverty." Create a budget as a couple, and diligently track your income and expenses. Budgeting can help you make informed decisions that align with your financial goals and faith.

Avoiding Debt

Christian teaching encourages living within your means and avoiding debt. Romans 13:8 advises, "Let no debt remain outstanding, except the continuing debt to love one another." Work together to minimize and manage debt, and seek to live a life that honors your faith by making responsible financial choices.

Tithing and Giving Back

Tithing, or giving a portion of your income to the church and to charitable causes, is a fundamental practice for many Christian couples. Malachi 3:10 instructs, "Bring the whole tithe into the storehouse, that there may be food in my house." By tithing and giving, you demonstrate your faith and generosity.

Transparency and Accountability

Maintain transparency in your financial dealings. Share account information, statements, and financial plans with each other. Accountability fosters trust and mutual responsibility in managing your financial resources.

Planning for the Future

Ecclesiastes 7:12 reminds us, "Wisdom is a shelter as money is a shelter, but the advantage of knowledge is this: Wisdom preserves the life of its possessor." Plan for your financial future with wisdom. Consider savings, investments, and insurance as ways to ensure the well-being of your family and to honor your Christian responsibility.

Seeking Guidance

If financial issues become a source of tension in your marriage, consider seeking guidance from your church or a financial counselor who shares your Christian values. They can help you navigate financial challenges while maintaining your commitment to faith.

In a Christian marriage, financial stewardship is an opportunity to honor God through responsible and ethical management of your resources. By aligning your financial choices with your faith, you can create a stable and harmonious financial foundation that strengthens your partnership and supports your shared values. As you continue your journey together, may your financial decisions reflect the love, trust, and faith you hold dear.

7

Intimacy and Purity in Christian Marriage

Nurturing the Sacred Bond

Intimacy is an integral part of Christian marriage, and it encompasses far more than physical closeness. In this chapter, we explore the deeper meaning of intimacy in a Christian marriage, emphasizing purity, love, and the sanctity of the marital bond.

God's Design for Intimacy

The Bible teaches that the marital union is designed by God as a reflection of the profound intimacy between Christ and His Church. Ephesians 5:31-32 states, "For this reason, a man will leave his father and mother and be united to his wife, and the two will become one flesh. This is a profound mystery—but I am talking about Christ and the Church."

Physical Intimacy

Physical intimacy is a gift from God, meant to be cherished within the confines of marriage. 1 Corinthians 7:3-5 advises, "The husband should fulfill his marital duty to his wife, and likewise the wife to her husband. The wife does not have authority over her own body but yields it to her husband. In the same way, the husband does not have authority over his own body but yields it to his wife."

Emotional and Spiritual Intimacy

Christian intimacy extends beyond the physical. Emotional and spiritual intimacy is equally vital. It involves open and honest communication, trust, and shared spiritual journeys. In a Christian marriage, you strive to understand and nurture each other's souls as you walk together in faith.

Preserving Purity

Purity is a core Christian value, and it applies to physical, emotional, and mental aspects of intimacy. Hebrews 13:4 urges, "Marriage should be honored by all, and the marriage bed kept pure." Maintain a commitment to purity by protecting your marriage from outside influences and temptations that may threaten its sanctity.

Respecting Boundaries

In a Christian marriage, it's essential to establish and respect boundaries in your physical and emotional interactions. Understand each other's comfort zones and limitations, and honor these boundaries as an expression of love and respect.

Fidelity and Trust

Fidelity is a foundational principle of Christian marriage. The marriage covenant is a sacred promise of exclusive devotion. Proverbs 5:15-19 underscores the significance of faithfulness within marriage, describing the joy of a loving and faithful relationship.

Conflict and Reconciliation

Conflict can affect intimacy, but it can also be an opportunity for growth. Resolve conflicts with grace, keeping the lines of communication open and seeking reconciliation. Ephesians 4:32 advises, "Be kind and compassionate to one another, forgiving each other, just as in Christ God forgave you."

Counsel and Support

If issues surrounding intimacy become a challenge in your marriage, consider seeking counsel from your church or a Christian therapist. They can provide guidance and support as you navigate these sensitive matters.

In a Christian marriage, intimacy is a sacred and multi-faceted aspect of the marital bond. It involves nurturing physical, emotional, and spiritual closeness while maintaining purity and faithfulness. As you continue to walk this path together, may your intimate bond be a reflection of God's love and the beauty of the Christian marriage covenant.

8

Weathering Life's Seasons: The Beauty of Aging Together

Growing Old in Love and Faith

As the years pass, a Christian marriage becomes a testament to enduring love and faithfulness. The challenges and joys of aging together provide opportunities to deepen your relationship with your spouse and with God. In this chapter, we explore how to embrace the beauty of growing old as a couple in the light of your Christian faith.

The Beauty of Endurance

Christian marriage is a testament to the endurance of love. 1 Corinthians 13:7 teaches us that love "always protects, always trusts, always hopes, always perseveres." In the later years of marriage, you'll find your love has persevered through numerous trials and tribulations.

Reflecting on Life's Journey

As you grow older together, take time to reflect on the journey you've traveled. Celebrate the milestones you've reached and the challenges you've overcome.

Psalm 71:18 reminds us to "declare your power to the next generation, your mighty acts to all who are to come." Share your stories and wisdom with younger generations to inspire and guide them.

Caring for Each Other's Health

Health challenges can become more prevalent with age. As a Christian couple, it's important to care for each other's physical and mental well-being. Galatians 6:2 advises, "Carry each other's burdens, and in this way, you will fulfill the law of Christ." Support each other in seeking appropriate medical care and maintaining a healthy lifestyle.

Fulfilling God's Purpose in Your Senior Years

Your later years can be a time of renewed purpose. Consider how you can use your wisdom, experience, and resources to serve God and your community. Titus 2:3-5 highlights the value of older women teaching younger women. Mentoring and offering guidance to others can be a fulfilling way to live out your faith.

Embracing Changes and Challenges

Aging brings changes, both physical and emotional. It can be a time of adjustment and acceptance. Ecclesiastes 3:1 reminds us that "There is a time for everything, and a season for every activity under the heavens." Embrace the changing seasons of life with grace and faith, trusting that God is with you in every phase.

Eternal Love and Faithfulness

Christian marriage is a reflection of God's eternal love for His people. In your later years, this love and faithfulness become even more poignant. Psalm 145:4 says, "One generation commends your works to another; they tell of your mighty acts." Share the legacy of your love and faith with those who follow, leaving a lasting impact.

Seeking Spiritual Fulfillment

Your senior years provide an opportunity for increased spiritual fulfillment. Spend more time in prayer, scripture study, and community involvement. Continue to nurture your relationship with God as you grow older together.

Grace and Gratitude

Finally, approach the aging process with grace and gratitude. Be thankful for the enduring love you share with your spouse, and for the faith that has sustained you. As you age together, remember the words of Psalm 90:12, "Teach us to number our days, that we may gain a heart of wisdom." Every day is a gift, and the wisdom of your years together is a blessing.

In a Christian marriage, aging together is a beautiful and sacred journey. As you continue to walk this path, may your love deepen, your faith flourish, and your lives together be a testament to the enduring beauty of Christian marriage.

9

A Legacy of Love: Leaving a Lasting Impact

Passing on Your Faith and Love

A Christian marriage is not just a union of two people; it is a legacy of love, faith, and values that extends to future generations. In this chapter, we explore the importance of leaving a lasting impact through your Christian marriage and how to pass on the torch of faith and love to your children and grandchildren.

The Power of a Legacy

Proverbs 22:6 encourages parents to "Train up a child in the way he should go; even when he is old, he will not depart from it." Your Christian marriage has the power to shape the lives of your children and the generations that follow. It's a legacy that extends beyond your lifetime.

Sharing Your Story

Your marriage story is a powerful testimony of love and faithfulness. Sharing your experiences, both the triumphs and challenges, with your children and grandchildren can provide invaluable lessons. They can learn from your journey, understanding the importance of love, faith, and commitment in a Christian marriage.

Nurturing Faith in Your Children

Your Christian faith is a precious gift to pass on. Deuteronomy 6:7 instructs, "You shall teach [God's commands] diligently to your children, and shall talk of them when you sit in your house, and when you walk by the way, and when you lie down, and when you rise." Actively nurture your children's faith through prayer, scripture study, and by setting a godly example.

Incorporating Faith into Family Life

Make faith an integral part of your family life. Attend church services together, engage in Christian community activities, and encourage your children to be involved in youth groups and Sunday school. Creating a vibrant Christian environment at home strengthens your family's faith and bonds.

Serving Together

Participating in service and charitable activities as a family can instill a sense of purpose and compassion in your children. Galatians 5:13 reminds us to "serve one another in love." Serving others as a family can become a cherished tradition that reinforces the values of your Christian faith.

Open Communication

Maintain open lines of communication with your children and grandchildren. Encourage them to ask questions about their faith and your Christian marriage. Being approachable and willing to discuss matters of faith fosters a nurturing environment for their spiritual growth.

A LEGACY OF LOVE: LEAVING A LASTING IMPACT

Legacy of Love and Forgiveness

Just as you've demonstrated love and forgiveness in your Christian marriage, teach your children and grandchildren these values. Ephesians 4:32 encourages us to "Be kind to one another, tenderhearted, forgiving one another, as God in Christ forgave you." Show them how love and forgiveness can transform relationships and lives.

Praying for Future Generations

Pray for your children, grandchildren, and their descendants. Seek God's guidance and blessings for their faith and life's journey. Prayers are a powerful way to pass on your love and faith to the generations that follow.

In a Christian marriage, leaving a lasting impact is a sacred responsibility. Your legacy of love, faith, and values can shape the lives of your descendants for generations to come. As you continue to walk this path together, may your Christian marriage be a beacon of love and faith that shines brightly in the hearts of your family, enriching their lives and drawing them closer to God.

10

A Journey of Endless Discovery: Nurturing Your Christian Marriage

Growing Together in Love and Faith

As your Christian marriage unfolds, it's important to remember that the journey is one of endless discovery. In this final chapter, we reflect on how to nurture and sustain your marriage's love and faith, ensuring it remains a source of strength and joy throughout your lives.

Rekindling the Flame

Over time, the initial excitement of marriage can fade, and daily routines can take center stage. However, Christian marriage encourages you to rekindle the flame of love and passion. The Song of Solomon 7:10 beautifully illustrates this with, "I am my beloved's, and his desire is for me." Embrace the opportunity to rediscover each other and rekindle your love.

Growing Together Spiritually

Your faith journey is a continuous one. As individuals, and as a couple, you'll grow spiritually. Encourage each other's spiritual growth and engage in faith-building activities together. 2 Peter 3:18 encourages us to "grow in the grace and knowledge of our Lord and Savior Jesus Christ."

Date Nights and Quality Time

Carve out special moments for each other, whether through regular date nights or quality time spent together. Ecclesiastes 9:9 advises, "Enjoy life with your wife, whom you love, all the days of this meaningless life that God has given you under the sun." These moments of connection and intimacy are vital to a thriving Christian marriage.

Supporting Each Other's Dreams

In a Christian marriage, you support each other's dreams and aspirations. Encourage your spouse to pursue their passions and talents, knowing that your support is a source of strength for them.

Conflict Resolution with Grace

Conflict is a natural part of any relationship. Christian marriage emphasizes resolving conflicts with grace and humility. Matthew 18:15 guides us, "If your brother or sister sins, go and point out their fault, just between the two of you." Address conflicts privately and lovingly, seeking reconciliation.

The Art of Forgiveness

Forgiveness remains a cornerstone of Christian marriage. Colossians 3:13 encourages us to "Bear with each other and forgive one another if any of you has a grievance against someone." It's a practice that should be ongoing, demonstrating your commitment to love and grace.

Prayer and Devotion

Prayer remains a central component of your Christian marriage. It deepens your connection with each other and with God. Continue to pray for your marriage, your family, and each other's well-being.

Growth Through Challenges

Challenges are an inevitable part of life and marriage. However, they also provide opportunities for growth. Romans 8:28 assures us that "in all things, God works for the good of those who love Him." Embrace challenges as opportunities to strengthen your marriage and deepen your faith.

Counsel and Support

Don't hesitate to seek counsel or support from your Christian community or a professional when needed. Guidance and advice can provide valuable insights and tools to navigate the complexities of your Christian marriage.

In a Christian marriage, the journey is one of endless discovery, a continuous process of growth in love and faith. As you continue to walk this path together, may your marriage remain a source of strength, joy, and inspiration, serving as a living testimony to the enduring beauty of Christian love and faith.

11

Looking Back and Looking Forward: A Journey of Reflection and Hope

Celebrating Milestones and Embracing the Future

As your Christian marriage has evolved and matured, it's important to take moments to reflect on your journey thus far and to look ahead with hope and anticipation. In this chapter, we explore the significance of commemorating milestones and casting a vision for the future in the context of your faith and love.

Celebrating Your Love Story

Your love story is a testament to God's grace and your enduring commitment. Reflect on your journey, from the moment you first met to the present day. Consider celebrating significant anniversaries with meaningful rituals or ceremonies, renewing your commitment and expressing gratitude for the love you share.

Honoring Your Growth in Faith

As individuals and as a couple, your faith has deepened and evolved. Take time to acknowledge your spiritual journey, recognizing how far you've come in your relationship with God and each other. Psalm 138:8 assures us, "The Lord will vindicate me; your love, Lord, endures forever—do not abandon the works of your hands." Your growing faith is a testament to God's enduring love.

Setting New Goals and Visions

Looking forward, set new goals and visions for your marriage. Consider what you want to achieve individually and together, both in your relationship and in your service to others and to God. Habakkuk 2:2 advises, "Write down the revelation and make it plain on tablets so that a herald may run with it." Create a vision for your future that reflects your love and faith.

Blessing and Rededicating Your Marriage

At certain milestones, consider blessing and rededicating your marriage before God and your community. This act can symbolize your ongoing commitment to love and faith. It may be done privately or in the presence of loved ones who can offer support and encouragement.

Preparing for the Empty Nest

For some, a significant milestone may be the transition to an empty nest. As your children grow and leave home, take time to reflect on your roles as parents and embrace new opportunities for your marriage. Ecclesiastes 3:1 reminds us, "There is a time for everything, and a season for every activity under the heavens." Embrace the new season with grace and excitement.

Serving Together in New Ways

In your later years, explore how you can serve together in new ways. Whether through mentorship, community service, or mission work, find opportunities to use your love, wisdom, and faith to bless others.

Leaving a Legacy of Love and Faith

Consider the legacy you want to leave for your children and grandchildren. Be intentional about passing on your love, faith, and values, leaving an indelible mark on their hearts and souls.

Continued Support and Learning

Never stop seeking support and learning to enrich your Christian marriage. Attend marriage workshops, seek counsel from your church community, and continue to study scripture together. Your marriage is a living journey that requires ongoing nourishment and care.

In a Christian marriage, celebrating milestones and setting new visions for the future is a way to honor your love and faith. As you continue to walk this path together, may your reflections fill you with gratitude, and your vision inspire you with hope, guiding your love and faith to new heights and ever-deeper depths.

12

Love that Never Fades: The Legacy of a Christian Marriage

Eternal Impact and Everlasting Love

As your Christian marriage has unfolded over the years, it has created a legacy of love, faith, and commitment. In this final chapter, we delve into the lasting impact your marriage can have on your family, your community, and future generations, as well as how your love can be a reflection of God's love that never fades.

A Love that Endures

1 Corinthians 13:8 reminds us that "Love never fails." Your Christian marriage serves as a powerful testament to the enduring nature of love. As you reflect on your journey, recognize the love that has sustained you through all seasons of life.

Inspiring Future Generations

Your marriage leaves a legacy for your children and grandchildren. By demonstrating love, faith, and commitment, you inspire them to seek the same qualities in their own relationships. Your legacy is not just what you leave behind but how it continues to shape the hearts and lives of those who follow.

Serving as a Beacon of Hope

In a world often marked by strife and instability, your Christian marriage can serve as a beacon of hope. Colossians 3:14 encourages us to "put on love, which binds them all together in perfect unity." By showcasing love and unity, you become a source of inspiration and a living testimony of God's grace.

Nurturing Your Community

Your marriage can also have a positive impact on your community. By modeling love, respect, and compassion, you contribute to a more harmonious and supportive environment. Encourage community involvement and service to further the well-being of others.

The Gift of Faith and Wisdom

Your faith and wisdom, cultivated through years of love and commitment, are a valuable gift to share with others. Consider mentoring younger couples, offering guidance, and providing a source of strength during their own marital journeys.

Embracing the Joy of Giving

As you age together, you may find joy in giving back to your community and to charitable causes. Use your resources and wisdom to support those in need, serving as a reflection of Christ's love for the world.

Leaving an Eternal Mark

Eternal love and faith are at the core of a Christian marriage. 1 Corinthians 13:13 tells us, "And now these three remain: faith, hope, and love. But the greatest of these is love." Your love is not confined to this lifetime but extends to eternity, leaving a lasting mark on the hearts of those you have touched.

Embracing God's Love

Above all, your Christian marriage reflects the unconditional love of God. 1 John 4:16 reminds us, "So we have come to know and to believe the love that God has for us. God is love, and anyone who abides in love abides in God, and God abides in them." Your love is a reflection of God's divine love, a love that never fades, never wavers, and never ends.

In a Christian marriage, the legacy you leave is one of love, faith, and commitment that extends beyond your lifetime. As you conclude this chapter of your journey, may your love continue to shine as a beacon of hope and an enduring testament to the grace and love of God. Your legacy is one that touches hearts, inspires spirits, and continues to shape the world with the eternal love that never fades.

Book Summary: Walking the Path Together - Christian Marriage Advice

"Walking the Path Together: Christian Marriage Advice" is a comprehensive guide that illuminates the journey of a Christian marriage through twelve insightful chapters. This book navigates the complexities and joys of Christian matrimony, offering guidance, inspiration, and practical advice rooted in faith.

The book begins by establishing the foundational principles of a Christian marriage, emphasizing the importance of faith, love, and commitment as cornerstones of a strong and enduring union. It encourages couples to build their relationship upon these principles, ensuring a stable and lasting bond.

Each subsequent chapter addresses a specific aspect of married life, addressing the challenges and opportunities that arise throughout a marital journey. From communication and conflict resolution to intimacy, parenting, and financial stewardship, the book provides practical advice that aligns with Christian values.

One of the book's key themes is the notion of a Christian marriage as a lifelong journey of love, faith, and growth. It emphasizes the importance of nurturing the relationship throughout various stages of life and enduring the trials and joys together.

The book underscores the significance of spiritual connection in a Christian marriage, offering guidance on praying together, studying scripture, and seeking counsel within a Christian community. It shows how a strong spiritual foundation can strengthen the marital bond and provide guidance through challenges.

As the book progresses, it delves into the intricacies of parenting in a Christian home, navigating financial decisions, nurturing intimacy, and facing trials with unwavering faith. Each chapter provides a wealth of wisdom and practical tips for couples to apply in their own lives.

The latter chapters focus on the legacy of a Christian marriage, highlighting the importance of passing on love and faith to the next generation. The book encourages couples to reflect on their journey, celebrate milestones, and set new goals for their future together, all while embracing the enduring love and faithfulness that a Christian marriage represents.

In the final chapter, the book reminds readers that a Christian marriage leaves a lasting legacy that extends beyond this lifetime. It encourages couples to embrace their role as beacons of hope and love in their community and to reflect God's enduring love through their relationship.

"Walking the Path Together: Christian Marriage Advice" is a valuable resource for couples seeking to strengthen their Christian marriage. It provides a holistic approach to building a thriving, faith-filled relationship that can weather life's challenges and inspire future generations. This book is a guide to walking the path of a Christian marriage with love, faith, and unwavering commitment.